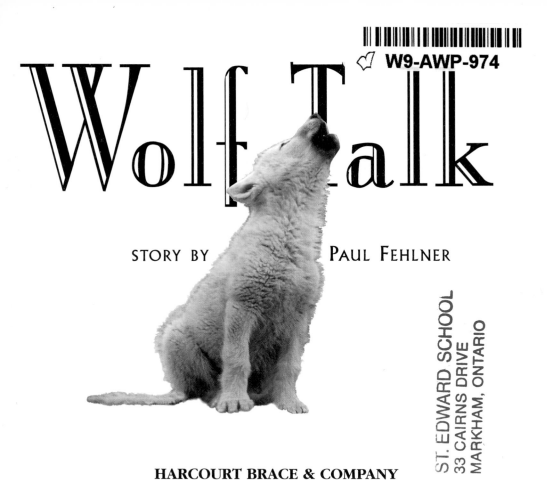

Wolf Talk

STORY BY   PAUL FEHLNER

HARCOURT BRACE & COMPANY

Orlando   Atlanta   Austin   Boston   San Francisco   Chicago   Dallas   New York
Toronto   London

Wolves tell each other a lot, just by the way they move or stand or touch. They watch each other carefully.

3

4

The leader holds his head high. The wolves around him know that he is the leader.

They keep their heads and tails down. This means, "You are our leader."

Most of the time the
wolves in the pack are
friendly to each other.
These wolves drag
their tails on the
ground. It looks like
they are sad, but
they are really happy
to see each other.

Sometimes wolves make sounds. An angry wolf growls and shows its teeth.

A mother wolf makes squeaking noises. This means that it is time to eat.

Wolves also howl to their pack. A loud howl may mean that there is good hunting.

Or it could mean, "Wait up for me!" Sometimes the pack will howl together.

The pack howl may sound
like a song—
    This is our home!
    Stay away!
    No company today!